GORILLA

ROBERT M. McCLUNG

illustrated by
IRENE BRADY

William Morrow and Company
New York · 1984

Printed in the United States of America.
10 9 8 7 6 5 4 3 2 1
Library of Congress Cataloging in Publication Data
McClung, Robert M.   Gorilla.
Bibliography: p. Summary: Examines the life of a band of gorillas in its natural mountain habitat and discusses the many dangers that threaten the existence of these peaceful and intelligent animals.
1. Gorillas—Juvenile literature.   [1. Gorillas] I. Brady, Irene, ill.   II. Title
QL737.P96M387   1984   599.88'44   84-718
ISBN 0-688-03875-1
ISBN 0-688-03876-X (lib. bdg.)

Contents

ONE

In the Shadow of the Volcano

Wreathed in clouds and mist, the Virunga Volcanoes of central Africa seems to float above the tropical lowland forest and plains. They rise in the Great Rift Valley, just north of Lake Kivu and south of the equator. There, three countries meet—Zaire, Uganda, and Rwanda. The two most westerly mountains of the Virunga Range are still active volcanoes, but the other six are dormant. They are the home of the few mountain gorillas that survive in the world today.

The night sky above the mountains was beginning to show the first glow of an April dawn. Foggy plumes of vapor swirled over the wooded slopes, and water dripped from the high branches of the trees. The eastern sky gradually changed to emerald green, then glowed yellow as the sun peeped over the crest of the range.

Birds began to call in the treetops, and a troop of red-tailed monkeys whooped a welcome to the returning day. A little red antelope, a forest duiker, left its bed under a

1

thorny patch of berry bushes and began to browse. A tiny sunbird, a flash of shimmering blue and green and red, darted overhead. Landing on a musungura, or wildrose tree, it began to probe the yellow blossoms for insects and nectar. Many of the mountain animals were starting the activities of another African day. The gorillas, too, were stirring in their leafy beds.

The first to awaken was Ingagi, the leader of the group. Sitting up, the giant male opened his mouth in a wide yawn, showing his long, sharp canine teeth. He rose and looked about, making sure that all was well with the others. Standing erect, Ingagi was five feet nine inches tall. His powerful body, with its broad chest and thickly muscled limbs, weighed almost 450 pounds. His legs were short and bowed, but his long, hairy arms hung to his knees. The thick coat of hair that covered his body was a shiny blue-black, except for a sweep of silvery gray hair across his lower back. That light hair marked him as an adult male gorilla, a silverback.

Ingagi's skin was velvety black. His head was massive, with flattened nostrils that were wide and flaring. Great bony ridges shaded his eyes, and another bony crest covered with gleaming black hair rose from the crown of his head. He was 24 years old, in the prime of life. Male gorillas become adults at 12 to 14 years of age, and may live 50 years or more.

Ingagi had been the leader of the group since its former

leader, his father, had died ten years before. With no other male members of the band ready to challenge him, Ingagi had succeeded naturally to the leadership. At present there were seven in the group.

A few feet away from him, a young female gorilla sat up in her bed of leaves and yawned. Kari was just 12 years old, the youngest of Ingagi's three mates. Sitting on her haunches, she peered about sleepily and scratched at an itchy spot under her left arm. Kari was much smaller than Ingagi. She was a big ape, nevertheless, and weighed about 250 pounds. Her belly was rounded and full, and her breasts were swollen. Kari was pregnant. She had been carrying the growing young one within her for the past eight months. Her first baby should be born very soon.

Suddenly she heard a snort from a nearby clump of bushes. Instantly wide-awake, Kari scrambled from her bed and loped over to Ingagi. The big silverback had risen to his hind legs again and was peering intently toward the spot from which the noise had come. As he watched, a herd of forest buffalo lumbered out of the underbrush— some 20 wild cattle with stocky, mud-caked bodies and wide, sweeping horns. Several red calves frisked among them. Ingagi hooted to alert the rest of his band.

The leader of the buffalo, a big bull, halted as soon as he saw the silverback and stared at him, eyes wide, fringed ears twitching back and forth. Ingagi grunted

loudly, then walked into a stand of bamboo to one side of the forest path. The other gorillas followed. They were giving the buffalo plenty of room to pass. The big bull hesitated for a moment, snorting and tossing his head. Then he headed on down the trail, leading the others past the gorillas. Soon the herd had disappeared among the trees.

After a few moments, the gorillas began to spread out, searching for their breakfast. Ingagi stood up one more time and peered about. Satisfied that there was no danger, he dropped to all fours, supporting his weight on his long forearms, the thick fingers knuckled under into huge fists. His body swayed from side to side as he walked across the clearing and sat down. Plucking a stalk of nettle, he nipped off several leaves with his teeth and began to chew them.

A big yellow-and-black butterfly fluttered toward the silverback and landed on the nettle he held in his fist. Uncoiling its tongue, it began to sip nectar from a blossom. Ingagi stopped chewing to watch the butterfly slowly opening and closing its wings just a few inches from his nose. He raised a finger and gently touched it. The butterfly took off and floated to another nettle plant a few feet away. Still following it with his eyes, Ingagi put several more leaves into his mouth and began to chew once more. Soon all of the gorilla band were foraging.

Oka, the oldest of the female gorillas and the highest-ranking of Ingagi's three mates, plucked a small shoot of bamboo and began to nibble at the stalk. Twenty-two years old, Oka had been Ingagi's mate ever since she had joined the group ten years before. Close beside her was her four-year-old son, Loki. Lively and full of mischief, he sampled a leaf, then leaped onto his mother's back and started to pull at the hair on her shoulder. Oka pulled him down and cuddled him for a moment before pushing him aside.

A few feet away lay 20-year-old Kivu, the second-ranked female of the band. Kivu's face was long and wrinkled, giving her a perpetually worried expression. Propping her head up on her arm and elbow, she began to munch on a stalk of wild celery.

Off to one side were two big male gorillas—Mbongo and Munidi. Mbongo was a 14-year-old silverback, almost as big as the leader. Born into the group, he had been just four years old when his half brother, Ingagi, became the leader. Now a young adult, Mbongo helped Ingagi protect the females and young. He would probably leave the band sometime soon to win mates and start a group of his own. Mbongo had only one good eye, his left one, as the result of a fight long ago with another gorilla. He also had a long, bare scar on his right arm.

Munidi, a slightly smaller male, was the older son of Ingagi and Oka. Nine years old, he was already bigger than any of the females. His back was black. It would be several years before he gained the silver-colored back of the adult male.

During the next two hours, the gorillas moved slowly through the thick growth, eating the choice leaves and tender shoots of plants as they traveled. They peeled off the tough outside layers from stalks of bamboo and ate the soft inner pith. They did the same with wild celery, smacking their lips over the tender hearts. They gathered juicy blackberries and other fruits, and popped them into their mouths with loud sucking noises.

The young blackback, Munidi, swaggered confidently from plant to plant, while four-year-old Loki scampered here and there, investigating everything in his path. The three adult females squabbled several times over who should get a particular morsel or occupy a certain spot. When the dispute got too loud, Ingagi silenced them with a glowering look and a short, abrupt bark.

In late morning, Ingagi signaled a halt and sat down with a loud grunt. Time had come for the midday rest. Munidi climbed into a tree, and Oka began to groom Loki. She checked his skin and hairy coat inch by inch, parting the fur quickly and expertly with her fingers, pausing briefly each time to examine the exposed area. Occasionally she would seize a loose flake with her fingers and pick it off.

Tired of his mother's grooming, Loki leaped away and slapped his chest playfully. He bounded onto a big log and hooted with excitement as he swung hand over hand into the branches of a huge, moss-covered tree. From the end of one swaying branch he leaped down onto his mother, who was just lying down to sleep. Then off he scuttled, to hurl himself recklessly onto the massive chest of his father, Ingagi. The big silverback roused himself to blink sleepily. He grunted and gently brushed the youngster aside.

The sun had already passed its high point overhead when Ingagi stirred and got up. It was time to move on. Grunting softly, he started off, and the others followed. One-eyed Mbongo acted as rear guard for the group, while Munidi patrolled first one side and then the other. Every now and then he would stop to hoot at a bird or to slap his chest.

The gorillas traveled slowly upward, following the sloping ridge of one spur of the mountain. They moved from the dense thickets of bamboo to a more open forest with scattered stands of mugeshi, or paperbark trees. These big trees had silvery bark and huge, buttressed trunks. Their wide-spreading branches were cushioned with yellow-green mosses and lichens, and dripped with ferns and pink orchids. A troop of golden monkeys passed overhead, chattering in the high branches when they sighted the gorillas.

In the lead, Ingagi felt faint vibrations in the hard-packed path they were traveling. He heard branches cracking ahead of him, then a shrill, trumpeting cry: elephants. Leaving the path, he led the others into a thicket of tall grass and scrub 100 yards to one side.

After a few moments, a herd of forest elephants swung into view, their gray-colored sides swaying in slow motion as they moved down the forest trail. From time to time they paused to strip leaves from the branches of trees and stuff them into their mouths.

Loki had seen elephants before, but he was still too young to respect them. He suddenly dashed away from his mother's side and ran forward to get a better look at the giant beasts. Oka barked sharply, calling him back, but the young gorilla paid no attention. Within a few seconds he was within 40 feet of the elephants and in full view of them.

A big cow elephant with a young one tagging at her heels was closest to him. When she saw Loki she flapped her great ears nervously, then raised her trunk and trumpeted loudly. The little elephant squealed with excitement and pressed close to its mother's side. Then it started toward Loki. It was curious, too.

Bellowing her displeasure, the mother elephant lowered her head and rumbled. Then she, too, began to move toward Loki. Realizing his danger at last, the young gorilla scrambled back toward his mother, who had come to rescue him. Together, the two quickly retreated. Urged on

by Ingagi, all of the gorillas promptly moved farther into the forest. The cow elephant trumpeted defiantly. Then, reassured, she turned and led her calf back to the herd.

In the late afternoon the gorillas came to a high mountain meadow nestled in the saddle between two opposing slopes. They would bed down here for the night. The sun was low and would soon disappear behind the mountains to the west. Plumes of orange-brown smoke curled skyward above the center of one of those mountains—a signal beacon visible many miles away.

Ingagi made his bed at the foot of a huge paperbark tree with a trunk nearly six feet in diameter. Bending the tall grasses and branches of bushes inward toward the center of the spot he had selected, the big silverback fashioned a crude nest. Breaking other branches and scooping up handfuls of leaves, he added them to the pile. In a few moments he had a comfortable, springy mattress nearly eight feet wide.

Mbongo built his nest some distance away, at the base of a wildrose tree. The three females made their beds on the ground between the two silverbacks, while young Loki constructed his sleeping platform in the fork of a tree, some 20 feet above his mother's ground nest. Adult gorillas usually make their nests on the ground, while youngsters often nest in the trees. But Munidi made his bed in a tree, too. It was a dozen feet off the ground, securely built between two stout branches of an old paper-bark tree.

By the time the sun had slipped down behind the western mountains, all of the gorillas were in their nests. The sky quickly changed from blue to violet to the black of night, except where the fires of the volcano cast flickering bands of glowing pink against the darkness. But the volcano was many miles away, and the gorillas were used to its glow.

With a sigh, Ingagi turned on his side and closed his eyes. Soon he was asleep. Kari, his youngest mate, had bedded down close to him. She was also drifting off to sleep when she heard the deep, throaty cough of a leopard on the prowl, faint in the depths of the forest. She turned uneasily, then settled herself again. Her baby was stirring within her. It would be born soon.

A tree hyrax, a small, guinea-piglike animal, whistled a few minutes later. Several bats dipped and swooped overhead, hunting for moths. But the gorillas neither heard nor saw them. They were fast asleep.

TWO

The Birth of Beni

Ingagi's band wandered over a territory that stretched across a half-dozen miles or more of the high saddle connecting Mounts Karisimbi and Visoke. The gorillas usually traveled no more than half a mile each day, for the vegetation they ate was abundant throughout the area.

There were many different kinds of terrain in the rugged slopes and valleys of the gorillas' territory. Thick stands of bamboo covered many of the lower slopes of the mountains. On the upper reaches these gave way to open woodlands where huge paperbark trees spread limbs cushioned with moss and ferns. Among them were scattered stands of wildrose trees with bright yellow blossoms. Further up the slopes, these woodlands blended into scrubby, twisted forests of giant heaths. In many places these were broken by mountain meadows with clumps of blackberries and beds of buttercups, violets, and other wild flowers. Above that, the trees dwindled and then disappeared entirely.

Other gorilla groups lived in the mountains, too. Several bands roamed areas that touched Ingagi's territory, and lone silverbacks sometimes traveled through it. Occasionally Ingagi's group met or passed these other gorillas in their wanderings. These encounters were usually peaceful, but not always.

One afternoon as the gorilla band fed on wild celery in a small clearing, they heard hoots from a nearby stand of bamboo. Another gorilla was calling. After a few moments a lone silverback as big as Ingagi stalked into view. Ingagi and the others stopped to watch the approaching stranger. Then Ingagi slowly walked toward him, placing himself between the strange male and the rest of the band.

The lone silverback ventured closer and closer, pausing from time to time to feed. When he was within 30 feet of Ingagi, he suddenly rose to his hind legs. He hooted and slapped his chest with open palms, beating a rapid tattoo. He stared hard at Ingagi, and the big silverback stared back. After a moment the stranger dropped to all fours and transferred his attention to Oka, who was sitting behind her mate, chewing on a stalk of celery. The strange silverback grunted at Oka. She glanced at him briefly, then looked away and continued eating. He ambled toward her, hooting softly.

Ingagi gave a sharp bark, then charged toward the challenging silverback and stopped just a few feet from him. The stranger stood his ground. Ingagi barked again, and the other members of his band began to move away, herded by Mbongo. The interloper watched them go but did not follow. Ingagi was blocking his way. After a few minutes the stranger turned and started off in the opposite direction.

That night, as Kari lay in the big bed she had fashioned for herself at the base of a tree, the baby stirred within her. Kari had left a neighboring group to join Ingagi's band just the year before. As the youngest of the adult females and the most recent arrival, she ranked third among them. The baby would strengthen her ties with the group. Kari's birth contractions began before dawn. An hour later, her baby was born.

Beni weighed just three and a half pounds at birth, about half the weight of most human babies. He had a tiny, wrinkled face and a spindly body thinly covered with fine, brownish black hair. His skin was gray, with pink showing on his face, the palms of his hands, and the soles of his feet. Beni's eyes were a soft, warm brown color, like those of his parents. His ears were big for his size and stuck out on either side of his head.

Kari carefully licked and cleaned the infant, then cuddled him in her lap. As the sun rose, she lifted him and tenderly cradled him to her breast. Soon Beni was nursing greedily. Kivu sat close by, watching him intently. Ingagi ambled over to examine his son. Soon every member of the band had inspected this new addition to the group. Their curiosity satisfied, they wandered off to feed.

Kari never let the infant away from her sight or touch. At night she slept with him cradled in her arms. During the day she carried him clutched to her belly, holding him with one arm while she walked on three limbs. Soon the baby would be able to cling tightly to his mother's fur by himself.

Beni thrived from the start. When he was six weeks old, he weighed six pounds, almost twice his birth weight. He clung to his mother most of the time but would creep about occasionally on his own. His baby teeth began to appear. Now he sometimes rode on his mother's back,

holding onto her fur with his strong little fingers and peering about as she moved through the forest.

Like any young animal, Beni began to take more notice of the outside world as he grew and developed. His eyes would follow a bright butterfly as it flitted past him, or a sunbird as it darted by on flashing wings. He heard insects droning in the trees and monkeys as they chattered and whooped overhead. He sniffed at plants and flowers, his nose wrinkling as he smelled the minty scent of a plant crushed under an elephant's broad hoof, the sweet perfume of an orchid, or the warm, familiar smell of his mother's body beside him at night. He quickly learned to recognize the powerful, musky odor of his father and the other adult males when they were angry or excited.

By the time he was four months old, Beni was beginning to experiment with plant food. Watching his mother, he would occasionally pluck a leaf or berry for himself and try it. Nettle leaves were bitter and prickly. Blackberries were sweet and juicy. The tender inner stalks of wild celery, he discovered, were crisp and good. But of all the foods he tried, he still liked his mother's milk best.

Sometimes he would sit up and pat his chest in imitation of the older males, then clap his hands together. Once in a while he would leave his mother and crawl off to investigate something on his own, but Kari did not usually let him get more than a few feet away from her.

As he gained weight and strength, however, she gradually relaxed her sharp vigil. When he was 6 months old, Beni weighed 12 pounds. He began to climb into the low branches of trees, but when he became too venturesome, his mother would pull him back to her. If he didn't get his way, he would sometimes bounce up and down, hitting the ground with his little fists and screaming with rage. At other times he would hit his chest with his palms and cry.

One morning Beni woke before dawn. He was warm and comfortable, snuggled as he was against his mother. But he was hungry, too. Groping for his mother's breast, he began to nurse. Kari murmured sleepily. She opened her eyes for a moment and peered at her young one, then closed them and went back to sleep. It was too early to get up.

The sun was just rising when Beni finished nursing. Leaving his mother, he started to crawl toward a nearby bush covered with white flowers. He watched a big green bird with bright red wing patches sail across the clearing and land on a mossy limb. For a moment the touraco teetered back and forth, the red feathers of its outstretched wings flashing like bright warning signals in the early morning sunlight. It started to hop from branch to branch, plucking and swallowing the small fruits it found.

Beni did not see the leopard crouched above him on a limb some 50 feet to one side. Its tawny yellow coat, spotted with black rosettes, blended with the sunshine and shadows of the early morning forest. The big cat's tail

twitched as it watched the baby gorilla approaching. Its muscles tensed as it gauged the distance and made ready to leap down. It could seize the infant and be off with an easy meal before the other gorillas realized what was happening.

Still half-asleep, Munidi lay in his nest in the crotch of a nearby tree. He gazed sleepily at a hornbill as it coasted in to a landing on a branch just ten feet away. Beyond the big bird he glimpsed another movement—the twitch of the leopard's tail. In an instant he was wide-awake. Screaming an alarm, Munidi scrambled out of his bed and climbed down to the ground as fast as he could. He had not yet noticed Beni sniffing at the nearby flowers.

Wakened by Munidi's cry, Ingagi scrambled out of his bed and roared. Kari got up, too, hooting with alarm as she ran over to Beni and scooped him up in her arms. At the same time, Ingagi saw the leopard and screamed a warning of his own.

On its lofty perch, the leopard drew back its lips and snarled. Its opportunity was gone, for it would not challenge an adult gorilla. Leaping from the limb, it bounded away through the forest.

THREE

The Raid

When he was a year old, Beni weighed 18 pounds. He was lively and alert, curious about everything that went on around him. Day by day he gained confidence and experience. He romped through the gorilla band as it fed, and played with Loki during the midday rest period. Loki was five years old now and much bigger and stronger than Beni. He was a friendly playmate, however. The two young gorillas would wrestle and roll about the forest floor, growling fiercely at one another in mock fury.

When Loki played too hard and sent Beni spinning, the yearling gorilla would screech with annoyance and run away. Sometimes he would chase after Loki in powerless fury, climbing up a fallen tree after him, or tussling with him on the ground. Cuffed too hard in a boxing match, he would run to his mother for comfort.

As a yearling, Beni usually rode on his mother's back when the band was on the move, holding on with one hand and grabbing at leaves and branches with the free one. Sometimes he walked beside her or wandered from one side of the gorilla group to the other, examining everything in his path.

There were new things to discover every day. One morning a tiny frog leaped in front of him, and Beni blinked with surprise. Recovering, he leaned over the little golden-eyed amphibian and touched it with his finger. The frog leaped again, disappearing into the grass.

That afternoon while he was playing, he found a baby duiker curled up under a bush. The little antelope peered up at him with dark, liquid eyes but did not move. Beni sniffed at the baby duiker, then stroked its satiny coat. The little animal flinched, but it still did not flee. Beni patted it gently for a moment, then ran after his mother.

When he tired of play or exploration, Beni would cuddle quietly against Kari while she groomed his thickening coat. She always checked him very carefully, parting his hair with her deft fingers and examining every inch of him from head to toe. Sometimes Beni attempted to groom his mother at the same time, searching for whatever he might find.

Beni could climb quite well by now. He often went into the trees, either by grasping low branches and pulling himself up, or by bracing the soles of his feet against the trunk and going upward hand over hand. He swung himself awkwardly from one branch to another or dangled on a strong vine as he investigated the new world of the treetops. Sometimes he went as high as 20 or 30 feet above the ground. Occasionally he lost his grip and fell, bouncing off the leafy branches as he dropped to the ground. Unhurt, but frustrated by his clumsiness, he would run to his mother for comfort.

Most of the adult gorillas did not climb very much, except during the season when one of their favorite foods, the fruit of the Pygeum tree, was ripe. Then every member of the group would climb into the trees to gather the red, plum-sized fruit. At other times, only Loki and Munidi spent much time aloft. They often went into the trees to eat or to build their beds. Sometimes they climbed just for the pleasure of it, or when they were playing a game of follow-the-leader.

Beni had long since begun to eat the vegetable food the others ate. He still nursed occasionally, however, whenever his mother would let him. He slept beside her at night in her big, leafy bed, cuddling against her furry side as he had done since he was born. Once in a while, he made a crude little bed of his own beside his mother's, gathering leaves and branches together, as she did.

In his play, Beni sometimes clambered onto his father's huge chest or belly while the silverback was snoozing. He would jump up and down on Ingagi's chest or tweak the long hair on his arms. Ingagi usually just blinked at such treatment, but if Beni became too much of a pest, the big gorilla would brush his son aside with a low grunt.

When Beni was 18 months old, Kivu, the second-ranked female of the band, gave birth to a female baby. Beni was very curious about this tiny new member of the group, a helpless little creature with soft brown eyes and big ears. He watched Kivu cradle the infant in her arms, holding it against her breast so it could nurse.

When the new baby, Coco, was just a few weeks old, Ingagi led the band down to the lower fringes of its territory. In this area the bamboo forest gave way to scrub and then to open areas and clearings on the lower slopes of the mountain. Here Bahutu farmers grew crops of grain and fruit, and Watutsi herdsmen sometimes tended cattle. As the human population of the region expanded every year, the Africans needed to clear more land for crops and grazing land for their cattle. In some parts of the mountains, broad fingers of cleared land thrust deeply upward into the bamboo forests.

Ingagi usually steered his band away from any place where they might meet human beings, although he had found many of them harmless enough. His vague feelings of mistrust had started many years before, when he was a youngster. A group of hunters had come upon his father's band high in the mountains. There had been a sudden, loud noise. His father had screamed in pain and clawed at his shoulder, where a bullet had lodged. Other shots had followed in quick succession as the gorillas raced away through the underbrush. They were frightened by the strange power that human beings had, by their ability to make loud noises that could injure or kill from a distance.

Mbongo had reason to mistrust humans, too. The scar on his arm was the result of a spear wound inflicted by a hunter some years before, when he was a blackback.

In spite of their mistrust, Ingagi's band bedded down one moonlit night at the lower edge of the bamboo forest. Not far below them was a grove of plantain, or banana, trees planted by farmers who lived in a tiny village near the base of the mountain. The hearts of banana plants are a rare delicacy to gorillas. The big apes love to strip the giant leaves and stalks from these trees and eat the tender pith inside the heart of the plant.

When the gorillas woke the next morning, Ingagi stalked slowly to the edge of the stand of bamboo and scrub. He peered down at the open slopes and listened for unusual noises. All seemed quiet in the banana plantation below. He grunted softly, and the gorilla group headed toward the grove of trees. Ingagi led the way while Mbongo and Munidi patrolled either side of the band. Beni walked beside his mother. Kivu followed close behind, clutching the baby Coco to her breast.

In a few minutes the gorillas reached the banana grove and began to strip the huge leaves from the trees and nibble the tender hearts of the plants. They had been feeding for almost half an hour when they heard shouts and the sounds of dogs barking from farther down the slope.

Ingagi sounded a warning to the others. Then he and the other two big males turned to face the danger. The females and young began to scramble back toward the sheltering forest. Beni could smell the powerful, musky scent of the two silverbacks and the blackback, always stronger when they were excited. He clung tightly to his mother's rump as she fled. Looking back, he could see several dogs and a band of humans waving spears and clubs as they advanced toward the male gorillas.

One of the dogs, more daring than the others, leaped to the attack. It sprang at Mbongo, but the big gorilla sent the dog spinning through the air with one sweep of his arm. The dog yelped with pain as it crashed to the ground and limped to the rear. Other dogs were attacking now, and the men with spears and clubs were close behind.

Ingagi screamed his defiance as he brushed one dog away. He charged toward the men, stopping just a few feet in front of them. Rearing up, he roared and beat a rapid tattoo on his chest with his open palms. Then Mbongo charged, too. The line of men wavered and fell back.

One man hurled his spear at Mbongo, and the sharp metal point plowed a deep, bloody furrow across his left arm. Mbongo screamed with pain. Rushing forward, he plucked a spear from another African's hand and splintered it. The man turned to run. As he did, Ingagi charged and bowled him over. Then he bit the man on the shoulder, cutting deep slashes with his long canine teeth. Other men rushed forward to help the wounded man, and Ingagi dropped his victim and retreated.

By now the females and young gorillas had reached the safety of the forest. Mbongo was hobbling toward it as fast as he could go on three limbs, blood streaming from his arm. Ingagi uttered one last scream of defiance and headed up the slope to join the others. The skirmish was over. Gorillas fight human beings, as he and the others had, only when they are attacked first or surprised.

Mbongo was not seriously hurt, and his wound soon healed. But now he had a long, jagged streak of naked skin on each arm. One scar was old, the other new. Both were the result of encounters with human beings.

FOUR

The Challenge

In early September the rains came again, ending the dry days of summer. There were several showers daily and sometimes hard rainstorms mixed with hail. The gorillas often took shelter under thick bushes or in the hollow bases of giant paperbark trees as they waited for the downpour to end. Otherwise, they huddled miserably on the ground, protected only by leafy branches of overhanging trees.

At such times, Beni grimaced as he felt the hard-driven pellets of water or ice beating against his skin. He watched tiny rivulets of water trickle down his arm between the hairs, and licked the drops from his hands. He sheltered himself against his mother's vast bulk as much as he could. When the rain finally stopped and the sun peeped out briefly between the low clouds, the warmth felt good.

For most of every day, clouds drifted through the valleys below the gorillas, and misty vapor whirled all about them. Every morning hoarfrost lay in the clearings, and the highest peaks of the mountains sometimes glistened white with snow. At night, however, the western skies still flickered with the fiery pink glow that came from the crater of Nyamlagira. Beyond that mountain stretched the endless wilderness of the Congo's tropical rain forest.

Just as the gorillas seldom ventured down into human territory, men seldom came far up into the Virunga Mountains. From time to time, however, the gorillas saw signs of them. One day they came upon a forest duiker caught in a snare. The little animal lay on its side panting, one of its hind legs hoisted into the air by a thin loop of wire wrapped tightly around its ankle, just above the hoof. Attached to a flexible bamboo pole thrust into the ground, the sharp wire had cut so deeply into the antelope's flesh that blood oozed from the wound. The duiker had been hanging that way for several days, struggling to free itself. It would soon die.

Poachers, illegal hunters, had set the trap. The duiker had been caught when it stepped into the hidden noose and touched a peg, triggering the trap so that the bamboo pole sprang upward.

Several days after they had seen the trapped duiker, Ingagi's band spied a lone male gorilla following them. He was a blackback, somewhat smaller and younger than Munidi. The stranger made no attempt to join them. He merely followed them at a distance, stopping to eat or rest whenever Ingagi and the others did. When dusk approached, he made a bed for himself some distance from the group. Snuggled close to his mother, Beni gazed over to where the blackback was curled up on his bed of leaves. He clutched his mother's thick fur in his fingers, sniffing her familiar musky scent, feeling the reassuring warmth of her body.

The strange blackback remained with the group the next day. Walking with a limp, he followed the band at a distance when it left the overnight camp and began to forage. Ingagi was well aware that the stranger was following them, but he made no move to drive him away. He glanced at the newcomer from time to time, however, and when he did, the young blackback would look away. By this action, the stranger showed that he meant no harm, offered no threat.

The females were well aware of the stranger, too, but they paid little attention to him. Munidi and Loki were more curious. They stalked over to the blackback that second afternoon in order to inspect him at close range. Hooting softly, the outsider turned his head aside as they examined him. Beni headed for the stranger, too, but Kari grunted sharply at him and he turned back. He had gotten close enough, though, to see that the blackback limped because of a wound. His right ankle was ringed with a broad band of bare and inflamed skin like that of the duiker they had seen several days before. This gorilla had been caught in a similar snare but had somehow managed to escape.

Several days went by, and the newcomer remained with the group, always at a respectful distance. At last Ingagi ambled over to inspect the stranger himself. The smaller male turned his head aside as the big silverback approached; he then meekly lay down and waited. Ingagi walked up to the blackback and circled him. He carefully looked him over from all sides and sniffed at his wound. Then he sat down beside the other gorilla and began to groom him. This showed that he was accepting the little blackback.

Once Ingagi had shown his approval, the others accepted the stranger, too. That afternoon the young blackback walked beside Munidi at the edge of the band and fed beside him. In that way Rafiki became the newest member of the group.

When they pose no challenge to the leading silverback, individual gorillas of either sex are sometimes permitted to join an established group. Ordinarily, young male gorillas leave their parents' group as they approach adulthood. They either roam the forests as lone silverbacks or set out to win mates and establish groups of their own. Young females also leave the bands in which they grew up when they reach breeding age and seek mates in other groups.

A week after Rafiki had joined them, the group encountered another lone male gorilla. He was not a blackback, however. He was a big silverback, as tall and heavy as Ingagi. Having lost his group to a rival, he now roamed the forest by himself. This gorilla came swaggering out of the underbrush one morning while Ingagi's group was feeding. He stood on his hind legs to stare at them. Then, slapping his chest briefly, he dropped to his knuckles and walked toward Oka.

The matriarch hooted uncertainly, and Ingagi hastened over to face the intruder. The strange silverback barked sharply. Standing up once again, he began to beat his chest rapidly. Ingagi stood up, too. Opening his mouth as wide as he could, he showed his long, sharp canines. He pounded his own chest and screamed at the other, warning him to come no closer.

In reply, the challenger charged at Ingagi. He stopped abruptly just three feet from him, and the two stared into each other's eyes. Ingagi roared at the intruder. *Wraagh! Wraagh! Wraagh!* Beni, peering out from behind his mother's back, jumped up and down and hooted with excitement.

Ingagi gave a loud bark then lunged at the other silverback. In a moment the two big gorillas were rolling on the ground. They roared and screamed as they struggled, crushing the vegetation all around them. Ingagi sank his teeth into the other's shoulder, cutting the flesh to the bone. His opponent broke clear and scrambled away,

screaming with rage and pain. Ingagi lunged after him, and the lone silverback whirled about and roared his defiance. In a moment they were wrestling on the ground again, biting and screaming.

The challenger finally broke free and retreated a short distance. Ingagi followed, and the other wheeled about to defend himself. For a long moment the two big males faced each other, eye to eye, without moving. The challenger was the first to lower his gaze and back slowly away. He was acknowledging defeat. Ingagi barked sharply, then turned his back on his retreating opponent and stalked back toward his group. The stranger disappeared into the underbrush.

The gorillas did not stop at the usual time for the midday rest. Ingagi was irritable and keyed up after the morning's encounter. He barked gruffly at the females and young ones several times when they squabbled over choice morsels of food. Finally the band came to a small, open clearing. Ingagi grunted and sat down. This was where they would stop. But the leader did not lie at ease, as he usually did. He was still touchy and excited.

The big silverback suddenly rose to his feet. Strutting stiff-legged, he walked over to a small bush and plucked a single leaf from the tip of a branch. He began to hoot, slowly and softly at first, then gradually faster and louder. His excitement became intense. Beni stared wide-eyed as his father placed the leaf carefully between his lips. Rearing up, the silverback began to slap his massive chest with his open palms. Faster and faster, harder and harder. *Pok-pok-pok! Pok-pok-pok-pok-pok-pok-pok!* The tattoo of blows, accented by Ingagi's hoots, echoed throughout the clearing.

Beni watched the performance with wonder and a stirring of excitement. Five-year-old Loki was jumping up and down, and Mbongo, Munidi, and Rafiki were all affected by Ingagi's actions. They hooted softly and beat their chests as they watched.

The big gorilla snatched the leaf out of his mouth and tossed it into the air. Dropping to his knuckles, Ingagi stamped hard on the ground, then began to shuffle quickly sideways, like a crab. He slapped at the vegetation on either side of him and pulled up big clumps of grass, throwing them into the air. Finally he thumped the ground abruptly with one palm and plopped down in the grass. The display was over.

Immediately Ingagi was his usual calm and gentle self again. He did not often act this way, but after he did, his feelings of excitement and aggression seemed to be calmed. Sitting up, he plucked a stalk of thistle and nibbled at it. He groomed his left arm, picking off bits of leaves and specks of dirt. After a few moments he lay down and closed his eyes. Soon he was asleep.

FIVE

The Gorilla Watchers

One afternoon the three young males played follow-the-leader. Munidi, the leader, scrambled up the slanting trunk of a paperbark tree. Rafiki followed at his heels, and after him came five-year-old Loki. Munidi stopped on a cushion of moss and lichens 15 feet above the ground, hooting and beating his chest. Plucking a pink orchid, he put it between his teeth and swung out on a vine toward the limb of a nearby tree. The vine broke before the others could follow, and Munidi went crashing to the ground, landing unharmed in a leafy bush.

Beni watched them. He had tried to follow the others when the game started, but he could not keep up with them in their rough-and-tumble play. He was not yet two years old. He sat beside his mother as she groomed Kivu, who was nursing her baby, Coco. Not far away, Ingagi lay on his side, idly watching the younger males play. Finally the big silverback closed his eyes to take a nap.

Tired of doing nothing, Beni wandered away from

Kari. He crossed the small clearing in which they were camped and climbed into a small tree. Settling into a forked notch, he beat his chest and hooted softly. He watched a white-necked raven as it flew overhead. Then he heard a dove cooing and saw it feeding two scraggly nestlings in a flimsy nest above him. Interested at once, he scrambled higher into the tree and sat on a limb near the nest to watch them. Creeping closer, he touched one of the baby birds. The mother dove cried in alarm and took off on whistling wings. Startled, Beni backed away immediately.

A movement on the far side of the clearing caught his eye. There in the distance was a human. This one was a female with pale skin and long, straight hair. Beni watched as she lifted a black object with two shiny round eyes and held it in front of her face. The round, gleaming eyes were pointed straight at him.

Beni hooted with excitement. His mother looked up to make sure that he was all right. Then Beni hooted again, and his father was awakened from his nap. In a moment the whole band was aware of the human intruder. Kari barked sharply, and Beni reluctantly climbed down from his perch and ran over to her. At the same time, Ingagi stalked forward to get a better look at the human. He halted some distance away to inspect her. The woman lowered her eyes and slowly shook her head back and forth in a gesture of submission.

Ingagi stood up for a better look. Uncertain whether to treat this human as a threat or not, he thumped his chest several times with his open palms. Making up his mind, he dropped to his knuckles and roared, then charged straight at the woman. He stopped abruptly about a dozen feet from her. Again the observer lowered her eyes. She scratched herself under the arm and grunted. Ingagi looked at her suspiciously, curious to see what this strange human would do next. The woman broke off a small piece of bamboo and held the stalk up to her mouth. She tore at the outer bark with her teeth and ripped it off. Smacking her lips, she chewed at the tender inner fibers.

Ingagi stood up and slapped his chest again. He did not know what to make of this human female. She did not

seem to be afraid of him. She was acting the same way a friendly gorilla would act. Dropping to all fours, he made another short rush at her. The woman grunted softly again, then turned her face aside and waited. Unable to scare her away, Ingagi turned his back on the stranger and stalked off. He grunted to the others, and they all started off through the bamboo forest. The woman did not follow them.

Several days later they saw her again. She was watching from a distance as they fed. This time the band moved off without challenging her, and the stranger followed at a comfortable distance. Whenever the gorillas moved, she moved, too. When they stopped, so did she.

After several days of this, most of the gorilla group accepted the woman as a harmless follower. But Ingagi was still watchful and alert. Although he did not completely trust the stranger, he would not challenge her as long as she kept far enough away. When he settled himself for his midday nap, the others went about their usual rest-period activities—snoozing, grooming, or playing. The observer stayed at a respectful distance from the group, seemingly content to watch the gorillas through the shiny eyes of her binoculars. She usually disappeared an hour or so before dusk, when the gorillas were beginning to make their beds and settle down for the night.

Day after day the woman followed the band. Occasionally she would not be seen for several days at a time, but she always reappeared. She never challenged the gorillas. She just watched them.

Sometimes a second human accompanied her—a young, bearded male. The gorillas soon became accustomed to him, too. The younger members of the band were full of curiosity about these two humans. Many of their activities seemed very gorillalike. Others were quite different.

One day, while the gorillas were foraging, Munidi ventured very close to the two humans. He deliberately walked to within a few feet of them, then halted and pulled up a stalk of wild celery. Peeling off the outer layers, he began to chew at the inner parts. Copying his behavior, the woman and the young man broke off pieces of celery for themselves and began to eat them. Munidi scratched himself and belched. The man did the same. Not knowing what to make of them, Munidi finally ambled away. Did these two humans want to join the gorilla band?

During the noon rest several days later, Loki and Beni slowly walked over to where the woman lay on the ground. Loki stared at her for several minutes. The woman returned his look and hooted softly. Loki hesitated, then walked even closer, with Beni following just behind him.

The woman slowly stretched out one pale arm. Loki looked at it. Gathering courage, he advanced and touched the outstretched fingers with his own black ones. Made bold by Loki's action, Beni darted forward and touched the woman's hair. It felt smooth and cool. Then the two young gorillas fled, both of them hooting with excitement. They had made contact with one of the humans.

It wasn't long before other members of the band grew confident enough to venture closer to the gorilla watchers and to watch them in turn. The woman and the young man would grunt at the gorillas in a friendly manner and then make markings in their notebooks.

By now both Loki and Beni had lost all fear of the two humans. They often sat beside the woman while she groomed them or gave them bits of fruit to eat. The young gorillas explored her clothes and hair. They flipped through the pages of her notebook and picked up her binoculars, holding the two shiny black eyes up to their own, as they had seen the woman do.

Soon other members of the group gained the confidence to visit the humans, too. Even Kivu, carrying the infant Coco, finally ventured close to observe them. Like the others, she had lost her fear of the woman and young man. They meant no harm.

Only Ingagi, the big silverback, stayed aloof. He was not afraid of the humans. He tolerated them. But he kept his distance. Then one morning he walked stiff-legged toward the woman until he was just a few feet from her. The woman grunted in a friendly manner and scratched herself. Ingagi gravely studied every movement she made. He sniffed her human smell and watched as she broke off a stalk of wild celery and began to chew on it. She hooted softly.

Ingagi sat on his haunches and scratched his side. Then he, too, plucked a stem of celery and began to eat it. He was finally accepting these humans as harmless and friendly observers. They were not gorillas, but in many ways they were like them.

SIX

The Gorilla Hunters

When the rainy season had passed, the gorillas gradually moved several miles westward to the saddle between Mounts Mikeno and Karisimbi. Many Pygeum trees, the source of one of the gorilla's favorite foods, grew in this area. The whole band would climb high into the branches of the trees to eat their fill of the red, plum-sized fruit. They had not seen their human observers, the gorilla watchers, for a week or more.

The gorillas were still asleep one morning as the eastern sky began to brighten from emerald to yellow. A white-necked raven croaked hoarsely, and in the depths of the forest a thrush serenaded the return of the sun. Beni woke up and yawned. Then he snuggled against his mother's back and dozed once more.

When the sun appeared over the eastern slopes a few minutes later, Ingagi woke. The leader sat on his haunches and stretched. It was the beginning of another day. Then he heard a strange noise, far off in the forest,

and was instantly alert. He looked about and sniffed the air but noted nothing unusual. Still suspicious, he stood up. He heard the unfamiliar noise again. Peering intently into the shadows of the forest, he dimly glimpsed a line of brown mesh in the distance. The wall of netting was slowly moving through the trees. Almost at the same time, he saw another brown wall moving in from another side. Ingagi roared his alarm cry. Suddenly wakened, the other gorillas scrambled from their beds, hooting and screaming at one another.

A loud report like an explosion sounded; then an outburst of shouts and cries came from the lines of mesh moving toward the gorillas. Humans, native hunters, had been observing the gorillas unseen. Now they were surrounding them, closing in with walls of strong rope netting.

Ingagi stood up and roared, beating his chest with his fists in a drumroll of defiance. Behind him, the females and young milled about in confusion, running first one way and then another as they searched for an escape route. Ingagi screamed and charged at the closest group of men. Not far away, Mbongo, backed up by Munidi and Rafiki, challenged a second group.

The line of hunters in Ingagi's path momentarily wavered and fell back. The huge silverback reared up once more and roared, his long fangs gleaming in the early morning light. The men facing Mbongo hesitated, too.

Behind the big male gorillas, the females and young were still trying to get away. Kivu, with Coco clutched to her breast, scrambled through the underbrush toward an opening between the trees. Kari followed close behind, with Beni clutching tightly to the fur on her rump. Oka and Loki ran beside them.

Covering the females' retreat, Ingagi charged the hunters and knocked two of them over with a mighty blow. Several shots rang out. Ingagi staggered and fell, blood streaming from his face and chest. He screamed again and again as the wall of men and nets advanced. Another shot exploded in his face, and his screams ended in a gurgle. The big silverback tottered and fell forward with a low moan. He was dead.

A hundred yards away, Kari scrambled into the lower branches of a big tree and climbed steadily upward until she was more than 50 feet above the ground. Branches brushed Beni's face, and he clung desperately to his mother as she struggled upward. Reaching a fork where two strong limbs met, Kari settled into it with a sigh. Grasping a branch, Beni crawled off her back and sat down beside her.

Another shot sounded. Beni saw his mother sway backward and then slowly slump over to one side. Blood was oozing from a small hole in her chest. Her strong fingers relaxed their grip, and she fell from her high perch.

Bouncing off several lower branches, she hit the ground with a jarring thud and lay still.

Confused and terrified by what was happening, Beni watched several other members of the band struggling far beneath him. They were entangled under the folds of heavy netting that the hunters had thrown over them. Mbongo was ripping at the rope strands and screaming loudly. One of the men darted forward and thrust a spear into his side. Another fired his rifle point-blank into Mbongo's face. The silverback fell without another sound.

Kivu, still clutching Coco to her, had climbed high into a tree not far from the one in which Beni and his mother had taken refuge. Another shot rang out. Kivu shrieked in

pain, then fell back and plunged earthward through the branches. She landed with a loud thump at the base of the tree. Kivu lay on her back, dead. Coco still clung to her belly. The baby gorilla seemed dazed but otherwise unhurt.

Beni climbed higher. Beneath him, Munidi and Rafiki were still struggling under the heavy folds of netting. So were Oka and Loki. Shouting with excitement, the army of hunters closed in, their guns and spears raised and ready.

Suddenly a wide rip appeared in the netting. Munidi had torn it apart. Roaring with excitement, the blackback scrambled out from under the heavy folds and charged straight at the men. They scattered before him as he flung one hunter aside and bit another on the leg. Then Munidi ran into the underbrush, followed by Rafiki, Oka, and Loki.

The four gorillas were gone before the hunters could recover from their confusion. They had escaped. But four others of the group lay dead.

Beni watched as several of the men approached the spot where Kivu's body lay at the base of a wildrose tree, the infant Coco still clinging to her breast. The baby gorilla cried in terror as the man pulled her from her mother, then whimpered pitifully as they carried her away.

Coco was a valuable prize for these illegal hunters. Gorilla hunting is against the law in the Virunga Mountains,

48

but poachers risked it because of the high profits they could make. Coco was alive and evidently uninjured. She would fetch a very good price from an animal dealer.

The poachers wanted Beni, too. They milled about beneath the tree, shouting at the young gorilla and throwing sticks at him. The hunters were trying to confuse him and make him tumble to the ground. Beni climbed even higher, clinging tightly to the slender, swaying branches.

At last the men retreated and disappeared among the trees. The forest became quiet, except for the distant chatter of a touraco. A quarter of an hour passed, and then half an hour. The forest seemed deserted. Beni peered down at his mother, lying so still beneath him. Slowly and cautiously he began to climb down. When he reached the ground, he scuttled over to the spot where Kari lay. He huddled close beside her and hooted softly, but she made no answering sound or movement. Her skin felt cold to his touch, and she stared at the sky with sightless eyes. Beni nestled against her furry side and whimpered.

Suddenly he heard shouts and saw the hunters rushing toward him. Before he could react, they threw a net over him and forced him to the ground. Beni, too, was captured.

SEVEN

To the Mountains of the Moon

Beni flailed under the folds of rope netting, but several hunters held him down easily with stout, forked sticks. When he stopped struggling at last, they lifted the net. One of the men held Beni's legs while another picked him up by the arms and thrust him into a small wooden cage with stout bars of bamboo on either side. The little gorilla weighed about 30 pounds now, and the cage was hardly big enough for him to sit up in.

Whimpering with fright, Beni grasped two of the bars with his fists and peered out. Nearby, several of the poachers were skinning the two slain silverbacks. Another was holding Coco. The baby gorilla clung to the poacher's khaki shirt and looked about, her eyes showing her bewilderment.

By midmorning the hunters had finished skinning the four dead gorillas. They folded the skins into bulky bundles, which four of the Africans balanced on their heads.

Two others thrust a thick pole through loops of rope in the top of Beni's cage. Shouldering the pole at both ends, they started off down the mountain, the cage swinging from side to side as they walked. The other men followed behind them, carrying the bundles of gorilla skins and the weapons, nets, and other supplies. One poacher still held Coco in his arms.

The procession walked through the open forest for half an hour, then through stands of tall bamboo and mountain meadows. While crossing the open areas, Beni sometimes caught a glimpse of the smoking volcano, Nyiragongo, far to the west. To the south, across distant fields of black lava, he could see the sparkling blue waters of a huge lake.

On the lower slopes of the mountain the thick stands of bamboo and occasional wild meadows gradually gave way to cleared land. The hunters passed through groves of plantains and other fruit, and then fields planted with maize and barley. Long-horned cattle, tended by tall Watutsi herdsmen clothed in white, grazed in several areas.

In early afternoon the caravan approached a little village near the base of the mountain. Some of the bamboo huts had roofs thatched with straw. Others were covered with giant plantain leaves. Scrawny chickens clucked and scratched in the dusty path, and goats and potbellied children stared at the strangers as they started to pass through the village. The gorilla hunters were not from this village

51

and did not want the villagers to know that they had two little gorillas with them. They covered Beni's cage with a ragged blanket to hide him, and the man carrying Coco hid her under a piece of burlap.

A mile beyond the village, they stopped to rest and eat in the shade of a big wild fig tree. Beni whimpered to himself. He was tired and bruised and thirsty, but at least the constant jarring motion of the cage had ceased. Suddenly a corner of the blanket covering his cage was lifted and Beni could see out. Several of the village children had approached to stare at the activities of the strangers, and one boy, more daring than the others, had lifted the covering over Beni's cage to peek in. Beni and the boy stared at

one another, their faces just a few inches apart. The little gorilla saw the other's eyes grow wide with amazement.

Whooping with excitement, the boy called to his companions in a shrill voice. Then he picked up a stick and poked at Beni through the bars. One of the poachers saw what he was doing and shouted, chasing him away. The boys and girls ran back toward the village, shrieking with laughter and chattering to one another in loud voices.

A few minutes later, a truck with a canvas roof and rolled-up canvas sides drove up. Two white men dressed in dusty khakis climbed out of the front seat. Both wore broad-brimmed hats to shield their faces from the sun. The older one, the leader, was big and fat. He had a red face and a black, drooping mustache. The younger man was slim and blond. Two black men climbed out of the back of the truck. Then all four of them walked over to inspect Beni and Coco. The mustachioed leader examined Beni while the younger white picked up Coco to check her over. Satisfied, he put her into a covered wicker basket that one of the Africans got from the rear of the truck.

The mustachioed white then talked to the chief native hunter. He gave him a small sack, and the African emptied it onto the ground. A handful of gold and silver coins spilled out. After counting them, the chief nodded. The payment was the price that they had agreed upon several days before for two young gorillas. The white traders did not want the gorilla skins now. The poachers would keep these and cure and dry them before offering them for sale.

The traders' two African helpers then put the two little gorillas under the sheltering canvas hood in the back of the truck and climbed in after them. The two whites got into the truck's front seat and off they went, lurching over the dried ruts of the rough dirt road. Before long they reached a wider and better road.

The traders planned to take the two gorillas to a big town several hundred miles away, on the banks of the Congo River. There they would sell them to an animal dealer, who in turn would ship them to some far-off country where they would probably be sold to a zoo. Although the capturing and selling of mountain gorillas is illegal, the dealer would make up forged papers authorizing the transport of the two animals. He hoped to sell them for a great deal of money.

For nearly two hours the truck lumbered along the dirt road, with the peaks of the Virunga Volcanoes looming above them to the south. They met very few cars, and when they did, the blacks covered Beni's cage with a piece of canvas to hide the young gorilla from curious eyes.

After passing through a small village, the road turned northward, away from the mountains. Soon they were traveling across a level plain. Peering out, Beni could see clouds of brown dust rising from the road behind him. On either side were tall stands of grass, now dry and yellowing since the rains had ended. A small flock of pink-and-gray doves rose from the side of the road with a whir of wings. In the far distance, a herd of elephants browsed on the lower branches of acacia trees.

In the late afternoon the road climbed into craggy highlands, winding its way through a thick forest of bamboo and then a more open stand of paperbark trees. At length it started to descend. Far beneath them, to the east, stretched the shimmering blue waters of another great lake. Ahead lay an open valley with a broad river winding through it. As they skirted the marshes that fringed the northern edge of the lake, vast clouds of water birds rose before them. The slanting rays of the late afternoon sun glinted off the white wings and pink backs of countless thousands of birds.

The truck passed a dead wildebeest lying by the side of the road. A flock of big gray vultures flapped heavily into the air. Then a small band of wildebeests ran across the road in front of the truck. Herds of bushbuck and waterbuck roamed across the many miles of grassland on the other side of the river.

Beyond the valley, many miles to the north and east, lay a group of mountains with five jagged, snow-covered peaks. The steep sides of the mountains were cut by many sparkling glaciers, their ice fields stained pink in the dying rays of the setting sun. These mountains were known as Ruwenzori, the Mountains of the Moon. Their glaciers fed streams that were the fabled source of the Nile River.

Soon it would be dusk, so the young white, who was driving, pulled the truck off the road and into a small grove of acacia trees. The Africans pitched the tents and prepared dinner while the two whites attempted to feed the two gorillas. The leader offered Beni a peeled banana, but the young gorilla turned his head away. Then he tried a mixture of boiled rice and beans, with similar results. Beni would not eat any of this unfamiliar food, in spite of his hunger.

The younger man poured milk from a flask into a bottle, put a nipple on it, and offered it to Coco. The baby gorilla made a few attempts to swallow, then sputtered and feebly pushed the bottle away. The man tried several more times, with no success. Cursing, he finally gave up. He sniffed at the milk in the bottle and made a face. The milk had soured. He then tried to feed Coco a mush made of powdered milk and water mixed with cornmeal, but Coco would not eat.

After the two whites had eaten their own supper, they sat by the fire drinking from a bottle of their own. From far away, Beni could hear deep, coughing roars—a lion at its kill. Finally the two whites crawled into their tent to sleep, leaving the Africans to take turns guarding the camp.

Dusk had long since turned to darkness. Beni listened to crickets chirping in the grass and a little owl hooting in a nearby tree. Still wide-awake, he was hungry and miserable. The campfire had died to glowing coals, and all four of the men slept, even the one who was on watch duty. Two bats fluttered overhead in zigzag flight. Beni curled up on the floor of his cage and dozed, whimpering softly to himself from time to time. He missed the comfort of his mother's warm body. Nearby, Coco lay in her basket. She did not make any sounds at all.

EIGHT

The Great Ituri Forest

The next morning, the traders left the long, broad valley and took a road leading to another small village. Beyond that lay the great Ituri Forest, a vast tropical rain forest that stretched hundreds of miles westward toward the heart of the Congo River Basin.

The green and yellow of the open valley gave way to stands of patchy scrub growth, and then to the dark forest. On either side of the road were towering trees— mahogany, teak, ebony, and many others—with thick, sculptured trunks that thrust skyward like great pillars. Only occasional shafts of sunlight pierced the thick foliage to lighten the gloom.

Barbets and bulbuls and other forest birds called from the branches, and little wagtails hopped along the sides of the road, their tails bobbing up and down as they searched for food. A band of sleek black-and-white Colobus monkeys with long, tufted tails chattered far overhead. The road became narrower and rougher, and the truck crossed several streams.

That night the men camped deep in the forest. The blacks kept the fire going all night, to discourage leopards, hyenas, and other meat-eaters that might be attracted to the campsite. A bush baby, a small, monkeylike animal, howled in the nearby trees, and a jackal barked deep in the forest. Beni could not sleep. He had eaten only a few bites of the unfamiliar food offered to him that evening, even though he was very hungry. Coco whimpered in her basket. She was growing steadily weaker.

After a hasty breakfast at dawn the next morning, the two whites tried once again to get the two little gorillas to eat. But Coco and Beni barely sampled the unappetizing food offered them. Finally the men packed their gear into the truck and made ready to continue the journey. But the truck would not start. The forest dampness was taking its toll. The two whites cursed and grumbled as they worked on the engine. They wanted to get to their destination as soon as possible. The baby female gorilla was not doing well. She would not eat and was becoming quite weak. She might die. In addition, the traders were worried that the villagers whose children had seen the little gorillas on the first day might have told government officials about them. Law officers might be following them right now.

At last the truck's engine roared to life, belching clouds

of blue smoke. Starting with a lurch, it headed on its way. Soon the travelers entered an area crisscrossed by many small streams. The current ran swiftly in some of them, with white water tumbling noisily down from the nearby hills and foaming around rocks and boulders. In others, the water moved slowly and silently. If a stream was shallow, with a smooth, hard bottom, the young white man drove the truck right across it, its wheels sometimes submerged to the hubcaps. But where the water was deep or the current swift, he cautiously edged the truck across a crude log bridge.

Beni stared through the bars of his cage at the water gliding past beneath the truck. He did not like water. Gorillas do not swim, and they venture into water only to wade across little brooks no more than a few inches deep. During Beni's two years of life, his band had crossed over slightly larger streams only twice, both times by walking single file on the trunks of great trees that had fallen across the streams.

Near midday, as they edged their way across one rickety bridge, Beni heard a loud cracking noise beneath him. The truck suddenly lurched sideways as one of the logs supporting the bridge gave way. Beni felt himself sliding backward, and before the blacks could prevent it the cage had toppled off the rear of the truck and into the water. Beni screamed with terror as his box crashed

against a boulder, splintering several of the bamboo bars. In a moment cold water was swirling all around him. He struggled desperately to escape.

One of the blacks leaped from the back of the truck into the stream, and as soon as the young trader had driven the truck onto solid land, he quickly followed. Wading through the foaming water, the two of them splashed over to where the cage lay wedged between two boulders. Together they lifted it onto the bank.

Chattering with fear, Beni bit the white trader's hand as the man began to lash rope in crisscross fashion over the broken bars of the cage. Muttering an oath, the young man snatched his hand away. He glared angrily at the bloody tooth marks and began to suck at them. After that, he was careful to keep his hands out of Beni's reach as he finished the repairs.

After the two men loaded Beni's cage back on the truck, the journey continued. Beni was wet and miserable. He whimpered and shivered, still upset from his fall into the stream. After he had dried off, however, he finally dozed.

In the early afternoon the travelers entered a section of the Ituri Forest where forest Pygmies, the Bambuti, lived. They saw no signs of the little people, however. Late in the day the truck arrived on the banks of a big river, several hundred yards wide. Here a ferry, an ancient steam-driven barge, carried the occasional cars and passengers from one side to the other. The ferryman was a wrinkled old African with a scraggly white beard and a blue yachting cap pushed back on his head. His only assistant was a grinning Pygmy dressed in khaki shorts. The little man of the forest was barely four and a half feet tall.

The white leader haggled for a few minutes with the ferryman, and then the younger white man drove the truck down a rough log ramp and onto the barge. There the old black and the Pygmy blocked the wheels and fastened chains to the front and rear of the truck to prevent it from rolling. The ferry was barely large enough for such a big vehicle.

As he cast off the lines, the Pygmy stared in amazement at the two little gorillas in the truck, then laughed with pleasure and excitement. The mustachioed white trader scowled fiercely at him and spoke harshly to his two black helpers. They had forgotten to hide Beni and Coco.

The ancient ferry began its trip, chugging noisily as it made its way across the river. At the tiller, the old African squinted, shading his eyes against the sun. A hippopotamus rose to the surface just ahead of the barge and blew lustily, then slowly sank out of sight. As the barge approached the log ramp on the opposite bank, several big crocodiles hissed and slid into the water from the slope where they had been sunning. After the boat was tied up, the truck lurched up the ramp and onto solid ground. Soon the Ituri Forest swallowed it up once more.

Dusk was approaching, and after a half-hour's drive the white leader steered the truck into a tiny clearing by the side of the road. They would stop here for the night. The two Africans quickly set up the tents and lit a fire. One of them tried to coax Coco into eating a lumpy mixture of powdered milk, water, and boiled rice, spooning it into her mouth as best he could. The baby gorilla ate a few spoonfuls but did not like this food and soon turned her head away. Clutching feebly at the man's shirt, she cried. The black tried again, adding several spoonfuls of sugar to the mixture and stirring some warm water into it. He felt sorry for the weak little gorilla. After much coaxing, Coco downed a half-cupful of the food.

The other African cautiously opened Beni's cage. The blond-haired white man quickly seized Beni and held his arms to either side while the black fastened a leather dog collar around the little gorilla's neck and attached a chain to it. Beni resisted, but the two men held him firmly. They did not want any more bites! The white trader fastened the other end of the chain around a tree trunk and quickly backed away.

Beni promptly scrambled to the end of the chain and tugged, trying to get free. He did not like the pressure around his neck. He walked around the tree in a circle, testing the extent of his freedom. He screamed in anger and frustration.

Approaching carefully, the black man set a broad leaf filled with cornmeal mush down in front of him and added a banana to it. Beni looked at the food for a moment, then scooped up a bit of it on his finger and sniffed it. He took a lick then turned away. The man offered a piece of bread soaked in the powdered milk mixture. After eyeing it suspiciously for a moment, Beni ate a few bites and nibbled at the banana. A short time later, the black and the young white man put him back in the cage for the night. Soon it would be dark.

Beni settled down to sleep. As he lay in his cage he spotted a slight movement in the underbrush at the edge of the clearing. A Pygmy was watching the camp activities. The little man stared at the camp for several minutes, then silently disappeared into the depths of the forest.

Meanwhile, the men ate their supper. Afterward, the two whites sat in front of their tent drinking from a bottle and arguing loudly. At last they disappeared inside, leaving the two blacks to stand watch, as before.

Soon everything was quiet, except for the buzz of insects and the occasional cry of a tree hyrax. Beni dozed fitfully, and Coco lay still in her basket. The two whites were soon snoring in the tent, but the blacks stayed by the fire and took turns sleeping and keeping watch. Near dawn, the man on watch fell asleep, too.

A slight movement wakened Beni. His cage was shaking. Three of the forest Pygmies stood around the cage. They had put a pole through the rope slings in the top of his cage, and two of them were lifting it to their shoulders. The third one picked up the basket holding Coco.

Balancing the basket on his head, the little man of the forest moved silently away from the camp, where the coals of last night's fire still glowed faintly. The two others followed, carrying the cage between them. Behind them, the two African helpers were stretched out on the ground, sound asleep, near the warm coals. In the tent, the two whites still snored. As the Pygmies went deeper into the forest, the sounds grew fainter, then faded away completely.

NINE

The Forest Pygmies

As the morning light grew stronger, Beni could see the Pygmies more clearly. The two Bambuti carrying his cage were so short that the bottom of the cage often bumped against the ground. Their skin was pale brown, and their only clothing were skimpy loincloths made of softened bark. Their hair was bunched into many tight little tufts. Each of the Pygmies was armed with a bow and a quiver of arrows. Each also had a hunting knife tucked into a leather scabbard at his side. One of them carried a spear, as well.

The sun was rising when they reached a small clearing where four other Bambuti were sitting around a campfire eating their breakfast. To one side were the carcasses of two red forest duikers and a heap of nets that the Pygmies had used in their hunting. When they spotted the three returning members of their hunting party carrying Beni and Coco, they greeted them with shouts of welcome. They crowded about the two little gorillas and examined them with many excited exclamations. The Pygmy crewman on the ferryboat had told the hunting party about the baby gorillas he had seen, and the Bambuti had decided to rescue them. Perhaps they would receive a reward for their return.

After all of the Pygmies had eaten, they broke camp and started the long trek back to their village, deep in the forest. Arriving about noon, they shouted to announce their return. The village, located in a tiny clearing, consisted of a circle of round huts, each no more than eight feet across and five feet high. Each hut was made of a framework of bent poles tied together at the top and covered with big, broad leaves that overlapped one another like shingles. A number of Pygmy women and children and several older men swarmed out of the huts to greet the returning hunters. They exclaimed excitedly when they saw Beni and Coco and crowded around to examine them.

Coco was whimpering with hunger and weakness, and the women saw how thin and listless she was. They chattered to one another for a moment, then one of them picked Coco up and held her in her arms. Another came forward with a small bowl made from half a dried gourd and filled it with steaming brown liquid from a nearby pot. After it had cooled, she held it up to the little gorilla's mouth and tilted it so that a bit of the warm soup trickled into her mouth. Coco sputtered and whimpered but swallowed the mixture. Encouraged, the woman offered her some more.

Another woman carrying a small child pushed closer to watch, and when the Pygmy baby saw the little gorilla it stretched a tiny hand out toward Coco and gurgled with pleasure. The Bambuti women were delighted. They laughed and clapped their hands.

One of the women scooped up some soft mush from another pot and offered it to Beni, thrusting her hand between the bamboo bars of his cage. She smiled at him as she did so and talked to him softly. Beni responded to the friendly face and voice. Pushing his face toward the woman, he slowly licked a bit of the food from her hand and then a bit more. But he still did not care very much for this strange food. The woman offered him a piece of raw sweet potato, and after a moment he began to chew at it. The Bambuti were happy to see the two little gorillas take some nourishment.

That afternoon, many of the villagers followed their chief and the hunters as they took Beni and Coco to a village a half-dozen miles away, where the Bantu towns-people lived. Most of these Bantu were farmers who traded fruit and grain to the little forest people in exchange for meat and skins, products of Bambuti nets and bows. The Bantu considered themselves the protectors and patrons of the Bambuti Pygmies who lived near them. The Pygmies, however, knew that they were free people who lived in and from the forest. It was their true protector.

When they arrived at the Bantu village, the Pygmies passed a number of huts with mud walls and thatched roofs. There were several larger houses, too, built of whitewashed clay bricks. Two-wheeled carts drawn by oxen and loaded with plantains and melons creaked past them. Tall Bantu men, some of them dressed in khaki shorts, others in dungarees and shirts, glanced up as the Pygmies passed and cried greetings to them. Women wrapped in bright-colored cloth walked by, carrying baskets of fruit or large clay pots of water on their heads. Children played in the street between the houses and shrieked with delight when they saw their friends, the Pygmies, and the little gorillas. By the time the Bambuti reached the house of the village headman, a crowd had gathered about them.

The headman was tall and stout. He examined Beni and Coco with much interest and asked the Pygmy chief many questions. He told him that he, too, had heard about the poachers who had killed four big gorillas in the Virunga Volcanoes three days before, even though that area was a protected sanctuary for gorillas. Rangers from the park had brought this news to the Bantu village just the day before. They said the poachers had taken two baby gorillas as well. A reward was offered for their safe return.

The Pygmy chief smiled and nodded his head vigorously in agreement with this news. He told the Bantu headman that the Pygmies would give the baby gorillas to him, and he could return them to the rangers. The reward would be divided between them. But the Pygmies wanted no money, their chief said. It was of no use to them. They wanted some new hunting knives and brightly colored cloth for their women.

The next morning the village headman and two local officials set off by car with Beni and Coco on the long journey back to the Virunga Volcanoes. Both gorillas were much stronger than they had been before the Pygmies rescued them. Coco had taken warm milk from a nursing bottle, and Beni, responding to kind treatment, had eaten some of the strange foods offered him.

At the ferry crossing, the villagers were met by two rangers from the Virunga Parc des Volcans. The exchange was made, and the rangers put Beni and Coco into the back of the truck they were driving. Off they went. Once again Beni saw Ruwenzori, the great group of snow-covered peaks that were the Mountains of the Moon. They drove through the broad valley with its herds of game and stopped for the night at a small camp and rest house near the shores of the blue lake with its clouds of water birds.

The next day they crossed the mountain pass and the grassy plains. Ahead lay the Virunga Volcanoes, the

mountains where Beni and ·Coco had lived all their lives. Beyond, to the west, were the familiar craters of Mounts Nyamlagira and Nyiragongo with their plumes of orange-brown smoke.

The rangers took a narrow road up the slope of Mount Karisimbi until they reached the saddle connecting it with Mount Mikeno. There the road ended. They were met by several Africans, who unloaded the young gorillas and led the way on the path up the mountainside. A half-hour

later, they arrived at a grassy meadow with several cabins in it. The Africans walked directly to the largest cabin, where a woman stood in the doorway. She was the scientist who had observed Ingagi's band for so many weeks. Behind her was the man who often accompanied her.

The woman lifted Beni in her arms. He clung to her and grunted softly. He recognized the woman, just as she recognized him. The young man took Coco, and they all went into the cabin. Beni and Coco were with old friends.

TEN

A New Band

They entered a big room with light streaming through several windows. On one side were doors leading to two smaller rooms. Beni clung to the woman's smock as she carried him across the room, all the while talking to him in a soft voice. She gently disengaged his fingers and set him on the floor.

The woman then went to a big food chest in a corner of the room and opened it. She took out a container and poured some milk into a pan. Meanwhile, the young man put Coco down. He stirred up the live coals in a little stove and added a few sticks of wood. Soon the milk was warming above the heat. When it was ready, he poured some into a bottle, attached a rubber nipple to it, and began to feed Coco. She sucked greedily.

Beni watched while the woman put some of the remaining milk into a big cup and added powdered cereal, honey, and several small, round objects from a jar. After stirring the mixture, she sat down, cross-legged, on the floor beside Beni. She scooped up a spoonful of the preparation and offered it to the little gorilla. Beni looked at the food suspiciously and sniffed it. Encouraged by the woman's coaxing, he took a timid bite. Swallowing, he licked his lips, then puckered them to ask for more. The woman continued to feed him, laughing to see him smack his lips after each swallow. Soon the cup was empty.

Supper over, she carried Beni to the other side of the room, where the young man was sponging Coco, bathing her in a big, shallow pan half-filled with warm water. Beni winced when his turn came and he was set down in the water. He tried to climb out of the pan, but the young man held him firmly. Finally he settled back and endured the water and the feel of the soapy sponge on his skin.

After a moment or two, the water began to feel good, like warm and gentle rain. When the bath was finished, the man toweled Beni dry and began to groom his fur with a big comb.

While all this was going on, several Africans brought in boughs of leafy limbs and carried them into one of the small rooms. Dusk was fast approaching, and the scientists soon took the two little gorillas into the room. The floor of the room was covered with branches of bamboo and other vegetation, and in one corner, beside a narrow cot, there was a big, leafy nest—a gorilla bed. The woman placed Beni in the middle of the bed of leaves, and the young man put Coco down beside him. Then he went away.

As twilight fell, the woman lay down on the cot. She talked softly to the two young gorillas, to reassure them in these new surroundings. Both Beni and Coco were tired from the events of the past several days. The room grew dark, and soon they were fast asleep.

When Beni woke, sun was streaming through the window of the bedroom. Coco was still asleep, but he could hear movements in the big room. Crawling out of his leafy bed, the young gorilla walked over to the door and peered through it. The woman was sitting at a table eating her breakfast, and one of the African helpers was stirring something on the stove. Another was sweeping the floor with a straw broom. The woman scientist smiled when she saw Beni and greeted him in a soft, friendly voice.

The little gorilla did not understand her words, but he watched with interest as the black man at the stove spooned some of the gruel warming there into the big cup he had eaten from the night before. Then the man began to spoon-feed him his breakfast.

A lonely wail sounded from the other room, and the woman went in to check on Coco, who had finally awakened. She brought the baby gorilla into the big room, and after a few minutes Coco was sucking contentedly at a nursing bottle. Soon the young bearded man came in.

"Now we'll try to find out how much you remember about gathering food for yourself," the woman scientist said to Beni. She picked him up in her arms and went outside, followed by the young man with Coco. The little female gorilla was too young to have learned how to gather much food on her own, but it would help if she were out in natural surroundings, too. She could watch the others as they looked for food, and their example would help her learn how to do it on her own. In that way, she would be better prepared when the time finally came to reintroduce her to a group of wild gorillas. She would soon be old enough to be weaned, as Beni already was.

The cabins were in a small open meadow, but the forest was just a short distance up the slope. Walking up to a thick stand of bamboo, the woman scientist sat down. Seizing a tender stalk, she broke it off and began carefully to peel off the leaves, laying bare the tender inner pith. Beni and Coco watched as the woman put the stalk into her mouth and nibbled at it. She offered some to Coco, but the baby turned away and the woman did not insist. She picked some wild celery next and offered part of it to Beni. He accepted the stalk and bit into it, chewing with satisfaction. A short time later, following the woman's lead, he picked some blackberries and ate them. After they returned to the cabin, the woman gave him a piece of plantain, and he ate that as well.

In the days and weeks that followed, the scientists and little gorillas went much farther afield. Sometimes they stayed out most of the day. Soon Beni was able to forage quite well, and little Coco was also beginning to learn how to find food for herself. She was getting better at tree climbing, too, and at gathering leaves and branches together to make a simple bed. Beni already knew these things. He and the woman scientist often built a nest at the base of some forest giant for their midday rest.

Late one afternoon, the four of them heard distant hoots, then rapid drumbeats that echoed through the trees. *Pok-pok-pok! Pok-pok-pok-pok-pok!* A big gorilla was slapping his chest somewhere up the slope. They moved in the direction of the sounds but did not hear the drumbeats again. Beni heard the faint crackling of branches ahead of them. Then there was silence. The gorilla group had gone on.

The next day, the scientists and the young gorillas set out to try to find the group. The humans hoped that the wild gorillas would accept Beni into their band. He was ready to return to his own kind now. He could find food on his own and could largely take care of himself.

They wandered through the forest all morning and soon found traces of the gorillas—trampled vegetation in an area where they had fed, beds in which they had slept the night before. About noon they heard grunts coming from over the next rise. The gorillas were not far away. Creeping closer, the two scientists and the little gorillas finally sighted the group. They sniffed the familiar musky scent of adult gorillas.

The group was led by a huge silverback. There were two blackbacks, too, and eight or ten females and young. The humans examined the band closely through their field glasses. Neither of them knew any of the animals in this group. It was evidently a new band that had just recently wandered into the area.

When he saw the other gorillas, Beni became excited. He hooted, and the whole group was immediately alert. They saw the two humans and the two little gorillas. The scientists bowed their heads and lowered their eyes to show that they were no threat. The young bearded man was holding Coco in his arms, but Beni was free. Hooting with excitement, he started to run toward the other gorillas.

Two adult females, one of them carrying a year-old baby on her rump, ran forward to meet Beni. They stopped when they were just a few feet away and stared intently at him. The gorilla with the baby seized Beni by the arm and tried to pull him toward her. At the same time, the second gorilla seized his other arm. Hooting with excitement, the two females tugged in opposite directions, each trying to pull Beni toward herself. Their excitement grew as they began to whoop and slap at one another. Screaming loudly, one of them slapped Beni.

Behind them, the big silverback barked. Roaring with indignation, he charged toward Beni and the two females. The hairy crest on his head bristled, and anger gleamed in his eyes. The two females quickly let go of Beni and scuttled back to their band. Just as quickly, Beni ran back to his human friends. The big silverback dropped to all fours and glared at the scientists for a moment. Then he turned his back on them and strode back to the other gorillas. He led them into a stand of bamboo, where they soon disappeared.

The two scientists sighed with relief as they started back to the cabin with the two young gorillas. This first attempt to return Beni to a wild gorilla group had failed, but at least he had not been injured.

A few days later, the scientists spotted another band of

gorillas in the area. They knew this one well. The gorillas in the group were used to being observed by humans. The scientists also knew that two members of Beni's old band had joined this group. In addition, the leader of the group was an old silverback with a calm and easy disposition, and one of the females had a baby just a few months old. Perhaps both Beni and Coco could find places with these gorillas.

The humans sat down with Beni and Coco some distance from this group to watch and wait. The gorillas were not disturbed to see the scientists, for they knew them. They were greatly interested in seeing the little gorillas with them, however, and approached closer to look them over.

The scientists grunted amiably as the gorillas approached, and the woman scratched herself and chewed at a stalk of grass. Beni hooted softly as the silverback stared long and hard at him. Then he saw two members of the group whom he recognized—Oka and Loki. Loki hooted with excitement when he spotted Beni and ran over to meet him. The old silverback looked on quietly as the two young males greeted one another. They sniffed one another and grunted softly. Then Loki put his arm around Beni, welcoming him.

At the same time, Oka went over to greet Coco, who was still with the two scientists. Grunting softly, Oka approached the two humans and sat down beside them. She examined Coco closely for a few moments, then began to groom her. A few minutes later, the female with the infant gorilla approached and sat down, too. This female was still nursing her baby. If she also accepted Coco, she might nurse her until the little female was fully able to forage for herself.

Coco hooted softly and then whimpered as the mother gorilla touched her. She crawled over to the big female and into her lap beside the younger baby. The female sniffed at Coco and began to groom her. She was accepting her. Two other females soon joined the group to examine Coco, too.

The two scientists stayed with the gorillas until late afternoon, while Beni and Coco were examined by every member of the band in turn. The humans followed the gorillas during their afternoon feeding, and when dusk approached, they watched them begin to make their beds for the night. Only then did they head back to camp, well satisfied that Beni and Coco were safe with a friendly group of wild gorillas.

Beni built himself a small leafy bed close to the bigger bed that Oka had made. Nearby, he saw that both Coco and the other baby were snuggled in the arms of the nursing mother gorilla. He listened to the old familiar sounds of insects droning in the treetops, and the distant call of a hyrax. Then he closed his eyes and went to sleep. He was back with his own kind.

The History
of an Endangered Species

"Nearly six feet high (he proved two inches shorter), with immense body, huge chest, and great muscular arms, with fiercely glaring, deep gray eyes, and a hellish expression of face, which seemed like nightmare vision; thus stood before us this king of the African forests.

"He was not afraid of us. He stood there, and beat his breast with his huge fists till it resounded like an immense bass drum, which is their mode of offering defiance; meantime giving vent to roar after roar . . ."

In this way the explorer Paul Du Chaillu described one of his encounters with a gorilla in the Congo forest in the 1850s. Du Chaillu had more firsthand experiences with gorillas than any other westerner of his time, but he did little to dispel the evil reputation that had long surrounded our nearest relative.

For 25 centuries, from the accounts in 470 B.C. of an early Phoenician encounter with hairy woodland animals they called "gorillae" in the course of a voyage along the west coast of Africa, myths and scattered bits of information about the gorilla and its aggressive temperament have been bandied about. Until recently, the real nature of the species was hidden and distorted by ignorance.

Few attempts were made to study the true nature of wild gorillas until 1896, when one scientist, R. L. Garner, had an iron cage placed in gorilla territory and sat in it patiently, day after day, waiting for the animals to come to him so that he could record their behavior. The gorillas did not oblige him.

Modern scientific studies of the species in the wild date back to 1921, when Carl Akeley, a naturalist, sculptor, and collector, traveled to Africa especially to study the gorillas of the Virunga Volcanoes and to gather the specimens needed for a museum group for the American Museum of Natural History in New York City. Akeley established his camp in a beautiful mountain meadow on the slopes of Mount Mikeno and called it Kabara, "the place of rest." Here he observed and studied gorillas, and collected five specimens for his museum exhibit.

He was so impressed with the beauty of the region where he worked that in 1925 he persuaded the Belgian government to set aside a large area in this part of the Belgian Congo as Albert National Park, a place where the animals and the environment would be protected from human disturbance. Yet in spite of Akeley's work, little was still known about how gorillas really lived and behaved in the wild.

The first extensive field study of wild gorillas was undertaken in 1959 in the Virunga Volcanoes. It was headed by John T. Emlen and George B. Schaller, of the University of Wisconsin, and continued by Schaller and his wife until the fall of 1960. They used as their headquarters the small cabin at Kabara on Mount Mikeno, where Carl Akeley had studied and collected gorillas nearly 40 years before. The results of Schaller's field studies were presented in a long, scholarly monograph and in a popular account, *The Year of the Gorilla*, published in 1964. His work added greatly to the understanding of the gorilla's ecology and temperament, and laid the foundation for most later field observations of wild gorillas. "Gorillas are eminently gentle and amiable creatures," he concluded from his observations, "and the dictum of peaceful coexistence is their way of life. In this man would do well to learn from the gorilla."

Schaller's conclusion is reinforced, for the most part, by the work of Dian Fossey, who came to Africa in 1963 and established a research center for studying gorillas, first at Kabara, and then at a new camp, Karisoke, on the slopes of Mount Visoke in Rwanda. She demonstrated the gorilla's basically peaceful nature through many thousands of hours of direct observations over a period of nearly 15 years. She became well acquainted with a number of different gorilla groups and individuals, and the animals in turn gradually grew to trust her. Many of them eventually approached her readily, sat beside her, and allowed her to pet and play with them. They obviously considered her a friend—which she was and is. Fossey has described her experiences in a number of magazine articles and in a book, *Gorillas in the Mist*, published in 1983.

Much of the background information and descriptions of gorilla life and behavior in this book are drawn from the writings of Schaller and Fossey. The chapter entitled "The Gorilla Watchers" is based upon field accounts of both scientists, and the events of the last chapter, "A New Band," were suggested by Fossey's experiences during similar real-life attempts to introduce young captured gorillas into wild groups.

There are three races of gorilla recognized today, although the western lowland form (*Gorilla gorilla gorilla*) was the only one known until this century. This subspecies ranges through the tropical rain forest of West Africa: from southern Nigeria through Cameroon, Mbini, and Gabon, inland about 500 miles almost to the Congo River and its tributary, the Ubangi. Separated from this western population by almost 700 miles of tropical rain forest, gorillas are also found in eastern Zaire (formerly the Belgian Congo) and the Virunga Mountains at the borders of Zaire, Uganda, and Rwanda. These eastern gorillas are recognized as two different forms: the eastern lowland gorilla (*Gorilla g. graueri*) and the mountain gorilla (*Gorilla g. beringei*). The mountain gorilla is distinguished from the lowland forms by its thicker and darker fur, narrower face, and a greater crest on the head of the adult male. Its range is restricted for the most part to the Virunga Volcanoes.

The areas of suitable living space for all three gorilla races have steadily shrunk, year after year, as forests are cut and more land is cleared for crops and pasture. Today, the gorilla is in serious danger of ultimate extinction in the wild. Years ago, the slaughter of wild gorillas during attempts to capture young animals was great. One of the most horrifying examples was the killing of 60 gorillas near Anguma, Zaire, in 1948, in order to capture 11 infants for sale. Of these, only one infant survived. Such atrocities are mostly in the past, but many wild gorillas are still killed today—for sale to individuals or zoos, for food, for trophies, and sometimes simply because they inhabit areas that human beings want for their own needs and requirements.

Today, the entire population of all three gorilla races may be less than 10,000 individuals, about the population of one small town of humans. Not a very big total when compared to the world population of *Homo sapiens*, which now approaches 4.5 billion. Fewer than 5,000 western lowland gorillas are thought to survive, and these few receive no protection in many areas where they are still found. There may be that many eastern lowland gorillas, too, but no one knows for sure.

As for the well-documented mountain gorilla, about 240 individuals still live in the Virunga Volcanoes. Some scientists say that these are all there are. Others believe that about 220 more mountain gorillas live in the Kahuzi-Biega National Park in Zaire, west of Lake Kivu, but these may be eastern lowland gorillas.

The regularity with which gorilla babies are now being born in captivity insures that the gorilla as a species will survive for the foreseeable future. Today, 10 to 20 baby gorillas, on the average, are born in the world's zoos each year. The first such birth occurred at the Zoological Garden of Columbus, Ohio, in December, 1956. In October, 1983, officials of the same zoo celebrated the birth there of twin gorillas, a rare occurrence. The total world population of zoo gorillas in 1980 was about 470, many of them born in captivity. However, zoo specimens of gorillas, or any wild animal, are no substitute for the preservation of that species in the wild. For that to happen, sufficient natural habitat must be preserved.

In 1978, one of Dian Fossey's most beloved gorilla friends, Digit, was killed by poachers. As a result of the public outcry, the Mountain Gorilla Project was organized in Rwanda and backed by a number of wildlife conservation organizations. Its purpose is to raise funds to promote gorilla conservation programs in the schools and among the local people of Rwanda, and to help with expenses for more park guards and equipment in that country's Parc Des Volcans. Guides now regularly take small groups of tourists on trips to the Virunga Volcanoes to observe gorilla groups that have become conditioned to the presence of human beings.

A real danger in such a program is the encouragement of more tourists in the area and the inevitable demand for similar services in remaining wild areas. Suitable gorilla habitat is still shrinking as the growing human population presses against the borders of the gorilla preserve. The eventual fate of this magnificent and peaceful animal remains very much in doubt.

Bibliography

Many books and articles have been consulted in the preparation of this book, but only a few written for the general public are listed below. Although these are aimed primarily at adults, they contain a great deal of general information and many illustrations that should be of interest to young readers who want to learn more about gorillas and other African animals and the lands in which they live.

AKELEY, MARY L. JOBE. *Carl Akeley's Africa*. New York: Dodd, Mead & Company, 1930. An interesting account of Carl Akeley's 1926 expedition to the Virunga Volcanoes to study and collect gorillas.

———. *Congo Eden*. New York: Dodd, Mead & Company, 1950. Mary Akeley returns to the scene of her husband's first expedition after gorillas. Much detailed information about the animals, plants, and people of the area.

DU CHAILLU, PAUL B. *Explorations and Adventures in Equatorial Africa*. New York: Harper & Brothers, 1871. A detailed travel story, telling of the adventures—some of them hair-raising, some of them exaggerated—in the exploration of the Congo River Basin.

FOSSEY, DIAN. *Gorillas in the Mist*. Boston: Houghton Mifflin Company, 1983. An excellent account of the author's 15-year study of mountain gorillas in the Virunga Volcanoes.

Fossey has also written articles about her experiences with mountain gorillas, which have appeared in the following issues of *National Geographic Magazine:* "Making Friends with Mountain Gorillas." January, 1970 (Vol. 137, No. 1), pp. 48-67; "More Years with Mountain Gorillas." October, 1971 (Vol. 140, No. 4), pp. 574-585; "The Imperiled Mountain Gorilla." April, 1981 (Vol. 159, No. 4), pp. 501-523.

SCHALLER, GEORGE B. *The Year of the Gorilla*. Chicago: The University of Chicago Press, 1964. A very illuminating account of the author's year studying the gorillas at Kabara, on the slopes of Mount Mikeno.

TURNBULL, COLIN M. *The Forest People*. New York: Simon and Schuster, 1961. A moving account of the author's life with the Ituri Forest Pygmies, and descriptions of their various activities.